# QUESTIONS AND ANSWERS
## ABOUT
# PLANET EARTH

Capella

This edition published in 2008 by Arcturus Publishing Limited,
26/27 Bickels Yard, 151-153 Bermondsey Street,
London SE1 3HA

ISBN 978-1-84837-158-3

Designers: Q2A India and Jane Hawkins
Editors: Ella Fern, Fiona Tulloch and Alex Woolf

Printed in China

# Contents

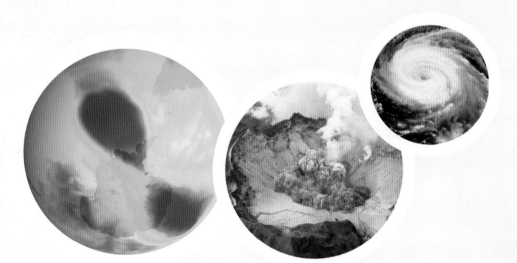

# Introduction

Earth is the only planet in the universe known to harbor life. It is surrounded by a protective blanket of air—the atmosphere—that allows us to breathe and prevents the planet from becoming too hot. The Earth's orbit around the Sun, and its tilted axis, are responsible for its weather, its climates and its seasons. The planet's often dramatic landforms—its mountains, valleys and caves—were formed over millions of years by erosion and the movement of the Earth's crust.

In this book, you can learn all about our home planet, its landscapes and oceans, and the violent natural disasters that frequently rage across its surface. Along the way, you will discover many fascinating facts. Why are days longer in summer and shorter in winter? How do volcanoes create caves? What was the worst earthquake in history? You will find the answers to these and many other questions in the pages of this book.

# Earth's Atmosphere

The protective blanket of air that covers the Earth is called the atmosphere. The Earth's atmosphere not only prevents too much heat from entering the planet, but also protects us from asteroids and meteors. The Earth's gravity helps hold the atmosphere in place.

## Quick Q's:

**1. What is a barometer?**

A barometer is used to measure the pressure in the atmosphere. When the pressure is high, the weather will be fine, sunny and still. When it is low, the weather will be stormy. When the pressure increases the liquid in the barometer is squeezed and when the pressure decreases it is released. This change is recorded.

**2. What is the exosphere?**

The exosphere is the final layer of the Earth's atmosphere. It extends way into outer space. The air in the exosphere is very thin, but the temperature is very high, because the Sun's rays shine directly on it.

**3. Why is the ozone layer important?**

The ozone layer is important because it stops harmful ultraviolet rays from the Sun from reaching the Earth. If the rays are allowed through the atmosphere, they can cause severe health problems like skin cancer. Chemicals called CFCs have made a hole in the ozone layer above the North and South Poles.

**Q** How many layers does the Earth's atmosphere have?

**A** The Earth's atmosphere is composed of several layers. These include the troposphere and the stratosphere. Each layer is divided according to the temperature and density of air in that layer.

**Q** What are the gases that make up the Earth's atmosphere?

**A** The Earth's atmosphere is composed of many gases. Nitrogen is the main gas found in the atmosphere. It accounts for about 78 percent and oxygen makes up 21 percent. The remaining one percent is a combination of carbon dioxide and water vapor. There are also very small amounts of trace gases like neon and helium that go to make up the Earth's atmosphere.

◄ **Long way out**
The outer layers of the atmosphere extend far into space.

**Q** What is the significance of the troposphere in the weather pattern?

**A** The troposphere is the layer closest to the Earth's surface, and it is here that weather is created. Air in the troposphere rises and falls, helping to form clouds, rain and snow. This layer stretches about 8–14.5 kilometers (5–9 miles) above sea level.

▼ **A warm blanket**
The Earth is protected by layers of gases. SOHO sends information about these layers back to Earth.

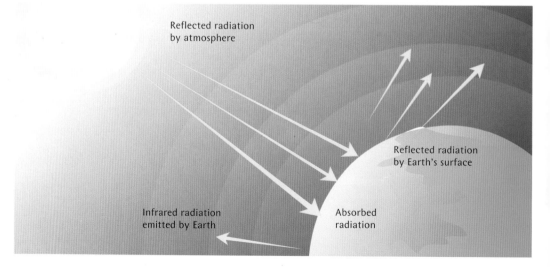

Reflected radiation by atmosphere

Reflected radiation by Earth's surface

Infrared radiation emitted by Earth

Absorbed radiation

**▲ Dangerous additions**
The pollution of the atmosphere by factories and vehicles is creating a dangerous hole in the protective ozone layer above the Earth and increasing the Earth's temperature. It also makes people fall ill more often.

**Q** How does the stratosphere help us?

**A** The stratosphere is the layer just above the troposphere. It extends upward from the troposphere to about 50 kilometers (31 miles) above the Earth's surface. Compared to the troposphere which is full of moisture, the stratosphere is dry. The stratosphere contains the ozone layer. Ozone absorbs harmful ultraviolet rays from the Sun.

**Q** Is the temperature the same in the different layers of the atmosphere?

**A** The temperature in the troposphere is between -52 and 17 °C (-62 to 62 °F). The temperature in the stratosphere is about -3 °C (26 °F). The next layer up, called the mesosphere, is very cold. The temperature here is as low as -93 °C (-135 °F). In the outer layers of the atmosphere the temperature starts to rise again, because there is more heat from the Sun. Temperatures in the outer layer can be as high as 1,727 °C (3,140 °F).

## When the Earth gets hotter

The atmosphere protects us from the Sun's heat by reflecting a lot of it back into space. However, some gases in the atmosphere trap some of this heat, keeping the Earth warm even at night. This process is called the greenhouse effect and the gases that cause it are known as greenhouse gases. These gases include water vapor, carbon dioxide, and CFCs. Humans are adding carbon dioxide and CFCs to the atmosphere all the time. Too much heat is being trapped, and the Earth is getting warmer. Global warming is leading to the melting of glaciers and polar ice caps and an alarming rise in sea levels. It will change the Earth as we know it.

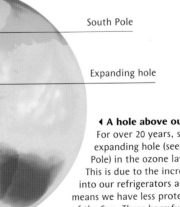

South Pole

Expanding hole

**Try these too...**

Seasons and Climate (10–11), Oceans (16–17), The Poles—The Arctic and Antarctica (28)

**◀ A hole above our heads**
For over 20 years, scientists have noticed an expanding hole (seen here in pink over the South Pole) in the ozone layer above each of the poles. This is due to the increasing use of chemicals that go into our refrigerators and aerosol cans. The hole means we have less protection from the ultraviolet rays of the Sun. These harmful rays can cause skin cancer.

# Seasons and Climate

The Earth not only orbits the Sun, but also rotates on its own axis as it does so. The Earth's axis is in fact tilted—meaning that neither of the Earth's poles faces the Sun directly. This tilted axis is responsible for weather and different climates.

## Quick Q's:

**1. What causes day and night?**

The Earth turning on its axis is responsible for day and night. At any time, half the Earth faces the Sun, where it is day, and half faces away, where it is night.

**2. Does the Sun really rise in the east?**

The Earth spins in an eastward direction. This makes the Sun appear as if it is rising in the east and setting in the west.

**3. Why are days longer in summer and shorter in winter?**

The angle at which sunlight falls on a particular area determines the length of day and night in that region. During summer the Sun stays above the horizon longer, making the days longer.

**4. What is the Coriolis effect?**

The wind moves to the right in the northern hemisphere and to the left in the southern hemisphere. This is called the Coriolis effect. It is caused by the Earth's rotation. It is mainly responsible for thunderstorms and hurricanes.

**Q** How is weather different from climate?

**A** Sunlight falls at varying angles onto the Earth's surface, heating up each of its regions differently. The difference in temperature eventually leads to different types of weather. A climate is when particular weather conditions prevail in a place for an extended period of time. So we can talk about the weather tomorrow or this month, but when we talk of climate we are talking of much longer time periods—decades or even centuries.

**Q** What is a season?

**A** A season is a period within a year defined by distinct weather. The tilt in the Earth's axis is responsible for seasons. In temperate and polar regions four seasons are recognized—spring, summer, autumn and winter. Some tropical and subtropical regions have a rainy season (sometimes called a monsoon season) and a dry season, while others have hot, rainy and cool seasons.

**Q** What are the factors that influence weather on the Earth?

**A** Temperature, rainfall, wind, cloud and atmospheric pressure are the main factors that influence weather patterns across the world. Wind is caused by the unequal heating of the Earth's surface. When the air above a certain region becomes warm and light, it rises and heavier, cooler air sweeps across from another area to take its place. This movement of air is called wind. Atmospheric pressure also affects the movement of wind, which always flows from a region of high pressure to that of low pressure. The difference in pressure between the two areas determines the speed with which the wind blows. If there is a small difference, we feel a breeze. If the difference is large, it leads to a storm. If the wind is flowing over a large water body such as a sea, it can pick up moisture and carry clouds and rain with it. Low pressure usually means stormy weather and rain, while high pressure usually means lots of sun and not much wind. There are other factors, such as the ocean currents created by the Earth's rotation, which also influence weather.

▼ **The blowing wind**
The wind always blows from an area of high pressure to an area of low pressure.

## Q How are clouds formed?

A The Sun's heat causes water in the oceans, rivers and lakes to evaporate and form water vapor. The warm water vapor rises upward, and as it rises, it cools down. As a result, the water vapor in the air condenses to form clouds containing tiny droplets of water. These droplets grow larger in size and finally fall down as rain. Sometimes, the temperature is so low that these droplets freeze into ice crystals and fall down as snow.

▶ **The water cycle**
All the water in the Earth's atmosphere, both on its surface and underground, is a part of the water cycle. The water is recycled again and again.

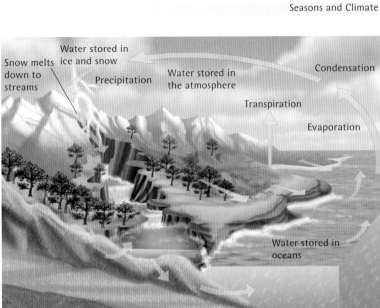

Snow melts down to streams · Water stored in ice and snow · Precipitation · Water stored in the atmosphere · Condensation · Transpiration · Evaporation · Water stored in oceans

▼ **Cold places**
The closer you are to the North or South Pole, the colder it is. Some animals have adapted so they can survive in the freezing temperatures.

## Q Which is the place on the Earth that has the coldest climate?

A The climate of Antarctica is the coldest on Earth. Nearly all of Antarctica is covered with an ice sheet about 2.5 kilometers thick. The lowest temperature recorded on this continent is -89.6 °C (-128.56 °F) at Vostok research station at the center of the East Antarctic Ice Sheet.

## Solstices and equinoxes

In the northern hemisphere the longest day falls during the summer, on 21 June, when the northern half of the Earth is tipped toward the Sun. This is known as the summer solstice. In the extreme north the Sun does not set at all during this period. During the winter solstice (22 December), the northern part of the Earth is tipped away from the Sun, resulting in the longest night of the year. On 23 September and 21 March the Earth is positioned in such a way that the length of day and night is equal (12 hours each). These days are known as the autumnal and spring equinoxes respectively.

### Try these too...

Earth's Atmosphere (8–9), Hurricanes and Tornadoes (22–23), Americas (24), Australia and Oceania (25), Europe (26), Africa (27), The Poles—The Arctic and Antarctica (28), Asia (29)

# Mountains, Valleys and Caves

Mountains are formed when two of the continental plates that make up the Earth's crust collide. The force caused by the collision pushes both plates (also called tectonic plates) upward, creating a mountain. Valleys and caves are also natural features created by erosion and the movement of the Earth's crust.

▲ **Climbing mountains**
Scientists climb mountains to study them.

## Quick Q's:

**1. Which is the highest mountain peak in the world?**

At a height of about 8,848 meters (29,028 feet) above sea level, Mount Everest is the highest peak in the world. It is a part of the Himalayan mountain range that was formed about 10–15 million years ago.

**2. How big is the Grand Canyon?**

The Grand Canyon is about 446 kilometers (277 miles) long and roughly 1.6 kilometers (1 mile) deep. It is made up of several layers of rock, each one older than the one above it.

**3. How are glacial valleys formed?**

When glaciers slowly flow downhill, they collect many pieces of rock on the way. These pieces scrape against the valley floor, digging deeper into it, until a U-shaped valley is formed.

**Q** **Can we live on mountains?**

**A** It is not easy to live on high mountains. The weather is extremely cold and not suitable for farming. At very high altitudes, oxygen levels are so low that it becomes difficult to breathe without an oxygen tank and mask.

**Q** **How are mountains different from plateaus?**

**A** Like a mountain, a plateau is higher than its surrounding area. However, plateaus have a flat top, while mountains have peaks. Like mountains, plateaus are formed when two continental plates collide, but erosion due to wind and water flattens the top. Plateaus are not as tall as mountains. In fact, some plateaus, such as the Tibetan Plateau, lie between two mountain ranges.

**Q** **How is a valley formed?**

**A** A valley is a low-lying area of land that is usually found at the foot of mountains or hills. The most common way valleys are formed is by the erosion of land from running water. River valleys are formed by the action of the river. As a river flows downhill, it cuts through the land like a knife. Over thousands of years the river erodes the land to form a valley, usually in the shape of a V. In contrast, valleys formed by glaciers are often U-shaped, because they are formed by rocks carried in the glacier that erode the soil.

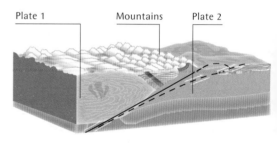

▲ **Forming a mountain**
Mountains are formed when two of the Earth's tectonic plates collide. The crust is forced up between the two plates, giving birth to the mountain range.

◄ **U-shaped valley**
Glaciers carry stones that scour out the soil, forming U-shaped valleys. Rivers, in contrast, usually form V-shaped valleys.

**Q** **What is a canyon?**

**A** A deep valley with cliffs on both sides is called a canyon. Sometimes a large river may run through a canyon. The Grand Canyon in Arizona, USA is the world's largest canyon. It was formed by the Colorado River. Millions of years ago, this region was covered by sea. Slowly, a part of the sea floor was pushed up to form a plateau. Over the years, rainwater collected to form a river. This river cut into the rocks on the plateau to form the canyon.

## Caves of lava

When volcanoes erupt, lava flows down the side of the volcano. The surface of the lava cools and becomes solid, while hot lava continues to flow underneath it. Once the eruption is over, there is a hollow tube, or cave, left behind underneath the hard crust of lava.

### Q What are caves?

A Caves are huge holes under the ground, in cliffs or under the sea. Caves can be formed in many ways. Most rock caves, especially limestone caves, are formed by rainwater that seeps into tiny cracks in the rocks. The rainwater contains minerals and chemicals that slowly causes the rock to dissolve, leaving behind a large hole. This process may take several thousand, or even a few million years.

### Q How are sea caves formed?

A Sea caves are formed by waves that wear away the rocks at the base of a cliff. These rocks are usually very weak and have tiny cracks in them. The continuous pounding of the waves causes the tiny cracks to widen and soon the rocks begin to crumble and form small hollows. These hollows keep expanding as sand, gravel and rocks brought by the waves erode their inner walls. Some sea caves are submerged during high tide and can only be seen when the water goes down at low tide.

▲ **Sea cave**
Sea caves are most common in areas where the rocks on the coast are soft.

### Try these too...

Other Landforms (14–15), Volcanoes (18–19), Earthquakes and Tsunamis (20–21), Americas (24), Australia and Oceania (25), Europe (26), Africa (27), Asia (29)

▼ **Rift in the Earth**
When two of the Earth's plates move away from each other, the soil covering them falls down and forms a rift valley. The rift valleys in East Africa now form a series of lakes.

Normal Faults

Earth's Crust

Mantle

### Q What is a rift valley?

A A rift valley is created when two tectonic plates pull away from each other, leaving a low space in the middle. The Great Rift Valley is the best known rift valley in the world. It covers a distance of over 6,000 kilometers (3,700 miles), stretching from northern Syria in West Asia to central Mozambique in East Africa. It began to form about 35 million years ago, when the African and Arabian tectonic plates began to pull apart. Even today it is still growing, as East Africa slowly separates from the rest of Africa.

# Other Landforms

Rivers, lakes and streams are natural bodies of water that are found across the world. When it rains or when snow on mountains melts, the water flows down the slopes, forming streams. Several streams join together to form a river. Small rivers drain into larger rivers. The water in rivers keeps flowing until it reaches the sea, though a few rivers hit very dry desert land and dry up.

## Quick Q's:

**1. Which is the largest freshwater lake in the world?**

Lake Superior, one of the Great Lakes of North America, is the largest freshwater lake in the world. This lake is over 560 kilometers (350 miles) long and about 257 kilometers (160 miles) wide.

**2. What is the Sahara known for?**

The Sahara is the largest hot desert in the world. Located in Africa, it spreads across Mauritania, Morocco, Mali, Algeria, Tunisia, Niger, Libya, Chad, Egypt, Sudan and Eritrea.

**3. Which is the longest river?**

The Nile is the longest river on Earth. It flows for 6,695 kilometers (4,184 miles).

**4. Why is Lake Baikal special?**

Lake Baikal in southern Siberia is the deepest lake in the world, with a maximum depth of 1,637 meters (5,371 feet). It has been around for almost 30 million years.

**Largest freshwater lake**
Lake Superior in North America is the largest freshwater lake in the world by area and the third largest by volume.

### Q How are lakes formed?

A Sometimes, rainwater collects in big hollows in the ground to form lakes. These hollows can be formed by the movement of the plates that make up the Earth's crust, or by moving glaciers. Lakes are also formed by landslides that leave huge depressions in the ground. Most lakes and rivers contain freshwater. In places containing a large amount of salt, lake water can be salty.

**◀ View from space**
This photograph, taken from an artificial satellite, shows Lake Baikal in southern Siberia. The size of the lake has been reduced in recent years, as more and more of its water is taken away for irrigation. It is considered to be one of the most serious problems in the region.

### Q What are waterfalls?

A Sometimes the surface over which a river flows drops suddenly. Then the water flows over to form a waterfall. There are different kinds of waterfalls. A cascade waterfall flows down a series of natural rock steps. There are no steps in a free-falling waterfall. In a fan waterfall, the water spreads out as it falls down. Angel Falls in Venezuela is the highest free-falling waterfall in the world. The water falls 807 meters (2,648 feet) without any interruption. Often, the sunlight falling over a waterfall creates a rainbow.

### Q Do rivers flood?

A Yes, they do. Rivers often overflow their banks and flood the land around them. This can happen when there has been a lot of rain or a lot of snow has melted in the mountain where the river starts its journey. Floods are often very destructive. They can damage crops and houses and kill people. But in the long run they can also do some good. They bring fresh soil down the river and spread it on the flooded land. Egyptian farmers have been dependent on the annual flooding of the Nile for thousands of years. The Amazon and the Ganges rivers regularly bring fertile soil to the agricultural areas downstream.

**▼ Longest river**
The ancient civilization of Egypt started along the banks of the Nile.

## Try these too...

Seasons and Climate (10–11), Mountains, Valleys and Caves (12–13), Americas (24), Australia and Oceania (25), Europe (26)

◀ **Largest desert**
The Sahara is the world's largest hot desert. It spreads right across northern Africa from the Atlantic Ocean in the west to the Red Sea in the east. Sand and rock cover most of the dry Sahara, but there are oases where people have lived for centuries.

## Q What is a desert?

**A** A desert is a dry region with very little rainfall. During the day, temperatures can rise above 50 °C (122 °F). However, nights in a desert can be extremely cold. Most deserts are covered with sand and rocks. Animals and plants that live in this habitat are specially adapted to life with little water and extreme changes in temperature.

## Q What are montane deserts?

**A** Some deserts, located at very high altitudes, are known as montane deserts. They are common in the Himalayas. Some, like the Tibetan Plateau, are relatively flat. Very few animals can survive the extreme cold and dryness, but the yak lives in Tibet.

## Q What is an oasis?

**A** For most part deserts are dry and have no water bodies. However, small springs with trees and plants growing around them can be found in certain places. These isolated regions are called oases. An oasis is vital for all forms of life in the desert.

## Cold desert

Most deserts are hot during the day, but some deserts are in the coldest parts of the Earth. Some cold deserts are covered in ice throughout the year, allowing very few plants to grow. Cold deserts are also not very suitable for animals. Few species can survive such extreme cold for long periods of time. Antarctica is the largest cold desert in the world. Patagonia in the southernmost part of South America and Gobi in Mongolia are also cold deserts.

# Oceans

Oceans occupy about 70 percent of the Earth's surface. There are five oceans in the world. They are the Atlantic, Pacific, Indian, Arctic and Antarctic oceans. The surface under the oceans is called the ocean floor. Like land, the ocean floor also has natural features like plains, valleys and mountains.

## Quick Q's:

**1. Which is the largest of all oceans?**

The Pacific Ocean is the world's largest and deepest ocean. It has an average depth of over 4,000 meters (13,100 feet). It has the world's deepest trench —the Mariana Trench near Japan. The Challenger Deep in the Mariana Trench is the deepest point on Earth —about 11,033 meters (36,200 feet) deep.

**2. What causes an ocean current?**

An ocean current is a mass of water that keeps moving in one direction. Surface currents are caused by wind and the Earth's rotation. Underwater currents are the result of differences in temperature and salt content of the water.

**3. What is a black smoker?**

When water seeps into the crust of the ocean floor through cracks, it may be heated by the magma below. As pressure builds up within the crust, the hot water shoots up through these cracks. These jets of warm water are often black due to their mineral content, so they are called black smokers.

**Q** Which ocean is also known as the Southern Ocean?

**A** The Antarctic Ocean is also called the Southern Ocean. Until recently, the Antarctic Ocean was considered to be a part of the other main oceans, as it was actually formed from parts of the Pacific, Atlantic and Indian oceans. In the year 2000, however, it was officially named the "Southern Ocean."

**Q** What is the ocean floor like?

**A** The ocean floor is far from flat. The edges of islands and continents gently slope into the surrounding water to form an area called a continental shelf that is higher than rest of the ocean floor. A continental shelf usually extends about 75 kilometers (47 miles) out to sea but some, like the Siberian shelf in the Arctic Ocean, can extend up to 1,500 kilometers (932 miles). The continental shelf contains large deposits of petroleum, natural gas and minerals. It also receives the most sunlight, so marine life thrives here. The point where the continental shelf starts to plunge steeply toward the deep ocean floor is called the continental slope. It is here that the deep canyons of the ocean are found.

West Wind Drift

▲ **Oceans of the world**
The five oceans of the world cover over 70 percent of the surface of the Earth.

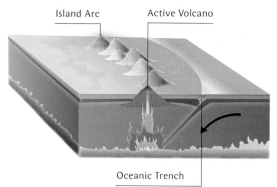

▲ **Not a flat floor**
The ocean floor has mountains and valleys. Some of the mountains are tall enough to rise above the surface and form islands.

**Q** What causes the formation of mountains and valleys on the ocean floor?

**A** Like the rest of the Earth, the ocean floor is divided into tectonic plates. The movement of these plates is responsible for features like ridges, trenches, and valleys. Ridges are formed when two plates drift apart. Boiling rock from inside the Earth, called magma, oozes out through the cracks between the plates and cools to form a ridge. Trenches are formed when a heavier plate sinks down under a lighter one.

◀ **Ocean currents**
The water in the oceans and seas is always in motion, due to the rotation of the Earth, the gravitational pull of the Sun and Moon, and the difference in temperature and salt content of the water. These movements form strong currents in the oceans, both at the surface and deep down.

## Q What is a mid-ocean ridge?

A The ridges on the ocean floor are connected to form a single chain called a mid-ocean ridge. The mid-ocean ridge is over 80,000 kilometers (50,000 miles) long and is the longest mountain chain on Earth. On average, these mountains lie about 2,500 meters (8,200 feet) below the ocean surface, with their peaks sometimes breaking above.

◄ **Mountains down there**
The mid-ocean ridge exists on the floor of all the oceans in the world. The diagram shows a part of the mid-Atlantic ridge, which extends below Iceland. Many volcanoes lie along the ridge.

## Q How are volcanic islands formed?

A Volcanoes under the sea are responsible for the formation of volcanic islands. As magma keeps oozing out of a volcano, it can collect, causing the volcano to grow and rise above the ocean surface as an island.

## Q What is special about the Hawaiian group of islands?

A Volcanic activity does not always take place near plate boundaries. There are some places deep inside the Earth that are much hotter than others. As a result, there is constant volcanic activity above these spots, known as hot spots. This activity leads to the formation of underwater volcanoes. The constant movement of tectonic plates eventually shifts the volcano away from the hot spot. Soon, another volcano is created in the area near the hot spot. This often leads to the formation of a chain of islands, such as the Hawaiian Islands.

## Q How are waves different from tides?

A Waves are caused by wind, while tides are the regular rise and fall of the ocean's surface caused by the gravitational pull of the Sun and the Moon on the water that is in the ocean. Waves are formed when winds blow over the surface of the ocean. Stronger winds create larger waves. The water in a wave normally moves in circles. As a wave approaches the land it is slowed down by the rising slope of the seabed. But it is the bottom portion of the wave that is slowed down. The top part of the wave keeps moving and crashes on to the shore as a breaker.

**Try these too...**

Earth's Atmosphere (8–9), Seasons and Climate (10–11), Volcanoes (18–19), Earthquakes and Tsunamis (20–21), Hurricanes and Tornadoes (22–23)

▼ **The breaker**
Breakers are higher when the seabed slopes down quickly from the shore. The beaches of Hawaii and Australia are famous for their high breakers.

### Feeling the heat

The temperature of the water from an underwater hot spring can be as high as 400 °C (752 °F). However, this water is rich in minerals, helping some unusual creatures like giant tubeworms and eyeless shrimps survive in an environment where nothing else can live.

# Volcanoes

A volcano is a mountain through which molten rock and gases erupt from the Earth's crust. Volcanoes are named after the Roman god of fire, Vulcan.

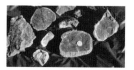

▲ **Volcanic rocks**
Hardened lava from volcanoes forms new rocks.

## Quick Q's:

**1. Which is the highest volcano on Earth?**

Mauna Loa in Hawaii is the highest volcano on Earth. It rises about 4 kilometers above sea level; below that, it extends to 5 kilometers down before it reaches the seabed. Its massive weight has pushed the volcano down a further 8 kilometers below the seabed! So Mauna Loa is 17 kilometers (56,000 feet) from its base to its summit.

**2. Which is the most active volcano?**

Mount St Helens in Washington State of USA is the most active volcano. It last erupted in 1980.

**3. What are geysers?**

Geysers are jets of hot water that erupt from the Earth. When water trickles down into the hot molten rock under the Earth's crust, it is heated up. As the water becomes hotter, the pressure builds up, finally causing it to spurt out.

## Q How are volcanoes formed?

**A** Volcanoes are formed by tectonic plates colliding with each other. The heavier plate is usually forced down below the lighter one, where part of it is melted by the heat of the crash. The melting plate forms magma or molten rock that collects below the surface of the Earth in magma chambers. As the amount of magma increases, the pressure inside the chamber rises. This creates a mountain, or volcano. The volcano has a cone, from which gases and lava may trickle out. When the pressure gets too high, the whole chamber explodes, ejecting the magma. This is a volcanic eruption.

▲ **Movements of the Earth**
The tectonic plates that cover the Earth can move in various ways, and are constantly rubbing against one another, sometimes violently.

## Q What are the various things that happen during a volcanic eruption?

**A** Magma, or molten rock, erupts through the surface of Earth during an eruption. Magma that comes out is called lava. It can be thick and slow moving or thin and fast. Pieces of rock and ash also erupt from the volcano. Pumice stone, a light rock full of air bubbles, is formed in an explosive volcanic eruption. These volcanic materials are called pyroclasts.

▲ **Hot water**
Old Faithful is a geyser of hot water in the Yellowstone National Park, USA. It erupts from the Earth every 90 minutes, on average.

## Q Do volcanoes erupt regularly?

**A** Volcanoes may be active, intermittent, dormant or extinct depending on how often they erupt. Active volcanoes erupt often. Intermittent volcanoes erupt at regular intervals. Dormant volcanoes have been inactive for a long time. They are the most dangerous because they are merely "sleeping" and can erupt without warning. Extinct volcanoes have not erupted for thousands of years. It is difficult to distinguish between dormant and extinct volcanoes because some volcanoes may remain quiet for a long time before suddenly becoming active again.

▼ **Active volcano**
Kilauea, in Hawaii, is considered the most active volcano in the world. It last erupted in 1983.

## Q What are the different types of volcanoes on the Earth?

A Volcanoes are classified according to their shapes and the type of material they are composed of. A shield volcano is a gentle sloping volcano that has long-lasting, gentle eruptions. Most of the volcanoes in the Hawaiian islands are shield volcanoes. A strato volcano is a steep volcano shaped like a cone. When it erupts, it emits gases, ash, pumice and lava. These volcanic eruptions are accompanied by deadly mudflows, making strato volcanoes the most dangerous among the volcanoes on Earth. Famous strato volcanoes include Mount Vesuvius in Italy and Mount Fuji in Japan.

▲ **The cone shape**
The cone-shaped volcano, known as a strato volcano, may be the most famous, but is only one of many types of volcano.

## Q Are there volcanoes under the sea?

A Volcanoes form under the sea in the same way as on land. When two oceanic plates collide, one may get pushed under the other. The heat generated by the crash causes one plate to melt and form magma. The hot magma rises and forms an underwater volcano, just as it does on land. The Vailulu volcano in Ta'u Island in the Pacific Ocean is an underwater volcano.

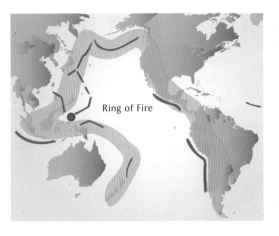

## Q What is the "ring of fire"?

A The area encircling the Pacific Ocean is called the ring of fire because most of the Earth's active volcanoes are located in a ring around it. The massive Pacific plate is expanding continuously at the edges of the ocean and hitting the other smaller plates next to it. The collisions cause frequent volcanic activity and earthquakes. The ring of fire stretches from New Zealand, along the eastern coastline of Asia and along the western coast of North and South America.

◀ **Ring of fire**
The ring of fire around the Pacific Ocean has been responsible for some of the most destructive volcanic eruptions and earthquakes in human history, including the 1906 San Francisco earthquake and the 1995 earthquake in Kobe, Japan. The biggest earthquake ever recorded was also in the ring of fire—the Great Chilean earthquake of 1960, 9.5 on the Richter scale.

### Try these too...

Oceans (16–17), Earthquakes and Tsunamis (20–21), Americas (24), Australia and Oceania (25), Europe (26), Africa (27), The Poles—The Arctic and Antarctica (28), Asia (29)

### An island disappears

One of the largest volcanic eruptions recorded in recent history occurred on the island of Krakatau in Indonesia in 1883. The eruption was so massive that most of the island disappeared into the sea (pale blue area between the two small islands). Over much of the world, the sky was dark with ash for days.

# Earthquakes and Tsunamis

The Earth is made up of a boiling hot, liquid center covered by a crust. This crust is broken into pieces called tectonic plates, which move around, sometimes colliding into each other. These collisions lead to earthquakes, some so small that they are hardly felt. But some earthquakes are so massive that they cause the ground to shake violently, destroying houses and killing people.

**◀ San Francisco 1906**
The notorious San Francisco earthquake in 1906 destroyed most of the large buildings in the city. Tramlines were ripped up as the roads buckled under them.

## Quick Q's:

**1. Which is the worst earthquake in history?**

In 1556, an earthquake struck three provinces in China. About 830,000 people were killed in the disaster. It was the worst earthquake in history.

**2. Can we predict earthquakes?**

No, we cannot. The movements of the Earth are too complex for us to be able to predict earthquakes. But we do know the lines along which the Earth's plates meet, so we know the areas that are more likely to have earthquakes.

**3. What is liquefaction?**

Liquefaction is caused by the violent shaking of the ground during an earthquake. Moist soil or sand turns into slurry, like quicksand. This liquid can suck in entire buildings.

**4. Is a tsunami the same as a tidal wave?**

A tsunami is different from a tidal wave. A tidal wave is generated by high winds, but a tsunami is caused by underwater earthquakes, landslides or volcanic eruptions.

**Q** Do earthquakes occur everywhere?

**A** Earthquakes usually occur along a region called a fault, where broken rocks under the Earth's surface rub against each other and cause tremors. Faults are marked by cracks on the Earth's surface, caused by the movement of tectonic plates. Most faults are located near the edges of the plates, but small faults can be found far away from the boundaries.

**Q** How do faults produce earthquakes?

**A** Faults allow the rock fragments that form the Earth's crust to move about. Over a period of time, plate movement builds up pressure, causing rocks along a fault to bend or break with a jolt. This sudden movement releases energy that moves through the surface of the Earth in the form of waves. This is an earthquake. The energy moves out in a circle from the point where the movement occurs.

**▶ Fault in the Earth**
The San Andreas Fault in California, USA, is one of the few faults in the Earth's surface that can actually be seen by any observer on the ground. Most of the other faults are covered by soil or water. These faults mark the lines on the Earth's surface where two tectonic plates of the Earth meet. As a result, areas around these faults are the ones most prone to volcanic activity and earthquakes.

**Q** Where is an earthquake most dangerous?

**A** The point inside the Earth where the rocks first begin to break is the focus of the earthquake. The point on the Earth's surface that lies directly above the focus is called the "epicenter." This is where the earthquake is strongest. In a major earthquake, the maximum damage takes place at the epicenter, and there is less damage as you get further away from it. The epicenter is directly above the hypocenter, the actual location of the energy released inside the Earth. Seismic waves ripple out from the hypocenter. After an earthquake, scientists can find the center by looking at the seismic wave data from three separate locations. The extent of the damage caused by an earthquake may also depend on the nature of the soil.

## Q Do earthquakes occur only on land?

A Earthquakes also occur under the ocean. Sometimes, massive earthquakes that start on the ocean floor can create giant, destructive waves called tsunamis. These waves move at great speeds (up to about 800 kilometers or 500 miles per hour) and can travel thousands of kilometers across the ocean. In deep water, the waves are not very high. They gain strength and height as they approach the shore. Tsunamis can be about 30 meters (98 feet) high. These huge waves break on to the shore with a great deal of force, bringing down trees and large buildings.

### When disaster strikes

On 26 December 2004, a tsunami spread across the Indian Ocean, killing over 250,000 people. The tsunami was caused by an underwater earthquake that occurred near the island of Sumatra, Indonesia. The tsunami hit the coasts of about 15 countries. Its effect was felt even in the southern tip of Africa, about 8,500 kilometers (5,300 miles) away from the epicenter of the earthquake!

Before

After

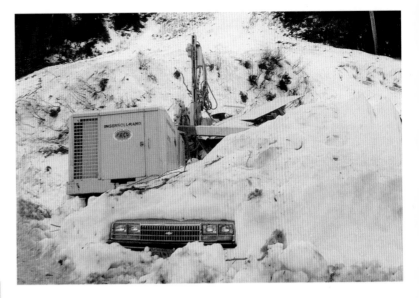

## Q Do earthquakes cause destruction every time they occur?

A Some earthquakes are extremely destructive. A strong quake can topple buildings and bridges, trapping people underneath them. If gas pipes and electrical wires break, they can start fires that rage for several days. Earthquakes can also cause landslides and avalanches. The violent shaking of the Earth sometimes loosens chunks of snow or mud that slide down the slopes of mountains and hills, burying houses and people under them.

## Q Can an earthquake be measured?

A Earthquakes are measured using the Richter scale. It was developed in 1935 by Charles Richter and Beno Gutenberg at the California Institute of Technology. This scale uses numbers from 1 to 10 to measure the intensity of an earthquake. Each increase of one point on the scale means a ten-fold increase in the strength of the earthquake. So a level 5.0 earthquake is ten times stronger than a level 4.0 earthquake. The Richter scale works by measuring vibrations around the epicenter of an earthquake.

▲ **Earthquake effect**
An earthquake can lead to a deadly avalanche or a landslide that can cause more damage than the original earthquake.

▲ **Old instrument**
The ancient Chinese invented an instrument that reacted to tremors in the Earth—a ball dropped from the mouth of the dragon into the mouth of a frog, warning people about a possible earthquake.

### Try these too...

Mountains, Valleys and Caves (12), Oceans (16–17), Volcanoes (18–19), Americas (24), Australia and Oceania (25), Asia (29)

# Hurricanes and Tornadoes

Sometimes the weather becomes wild. Blizzards, thunderstorms, hurricanes and heatwaves are some examples of extreme weather conditions. Such severe weather often causes a great deal of damage to both life and property. Hurricanes and tornadoes especially are very destructive.

## Quick Q's:

**1. Can hurricane winds be measured?**

Hurricanes are divided into five categories depending on their wind speeds. Category 5 hurricanes are the worst, causing maximum damage. Winds of a category 5 hurricane can reach speeds of about 250 kilometers per hour (155 miles per hour). Category 1 hurricanes are much weaker, and only travel at 119–153 kilometers per hour (74–95 miles per hour).

**2. What is a storm surge?**

Sometimes the strong winds of a hurricane can cause the water level in the ocean to rise. Huge waves hit the coast along with the storm, causing severe flooding. This is called a storm surge.

**3. What is the Fujita scale?**

The Fujita scale is used to measure the intensity of a tornado. It ranks tornadoes by the damage caused to man-made structures.

**4. How did tornadoes get their name?**

The word tornado is from the Spanish *tomear*, meaning "to turn."

### Q What is a hurricane?

A Hurricanes are large, violent storms that form over the ocean near the equator. These storms are accompanied by winds that travel at an average speed of about 119 kilometers per hour (74 miles per hour). Hurricanes usually occur between June and November.

▲ **Eye of the hurricane**
This satellite image clearly shows the eye of the hurricane, an area of calm in the middle of the storm.

### Q How does a hurricane form?

A When the air above the sea is heated it rises, creating an area of low pressure. Cooler wind moves in to take place of the warm air. The Earth's rotation causes the rising hot air to twist and form a cylinder. As the warm air rises higher, it cools down and forms huge thunderclouds and finally becomes a hurricane. Meanwhile, the cooler air at the bottom also becomes warm, adding more energy to the storm.

### Q What is the eye of a hurricane?

A The center of a hurricane is called the eye. The eye is an area of clear skies, light winds and no rain. It is also the warmest part of the storm and is surrounded by a wall of heavy rain and strong winds. People faced with a hurricane usually experience the heavy rain and strong winds first, then there is a period of calm as the eye passes over the area, followed by more stormy weather.

▼ **Huge destroyer**
In 2005, Hurricane Katrina, seen here in a satellite image, destroyed large parts of the city of New Orleans in the USA.

**Q** What is the worst hurricane on record?

**A** The hurricane that ripped through the Caribbean islands of Martinique, St. Eustatius and Barbados in October 1780 is the worst on record so far. It killed nearly 22,000 people. However, this hurricane does not have a name, because the practice of giving human names to major hurricanes started during World War II.

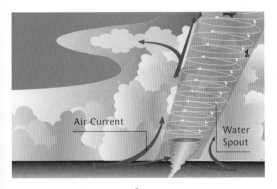

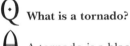
**▲ The making of a storm**
Warm air rises from the sea, taking water with it in the form of a funnel, and starting a storm.

**Q** What is a tornado?

**A** A tornado is a black, funnel-shaped storm that is highly destructive. These storms usually form where cold polar winds mix with warm, moist tropical winds. They start as rotating thunderstorms called supercells. Gradually the spinning wind in the supercell forms the funnel of a tornado. The wind in the funnel spins so fast that it sucks objects into it like a vacuum cleaner.

**Q** What is Tornado Alley?

**A** Tornado Alley is an area that extends across the Great Plains of the USA, from central Texas in the south to the border of Canada in the north. The conditions in this region are most suitable for the formation of severe tornadoes, which occur during spring and early summer.

## Chasing the storm

**Most of us would prefer to stay as far away as possible from all violent storms, especially hurricanes and tornadoes. Some people however, chase hurricanes and tornadoes. For these people,**  **confronting a storm is exciting. Storm chasers use special equipment to locate and follow storms. They usually have a well-equipped vehicle fitted with the latest technology, including cameras, radios, scanners and first-aid kits. The videos, photographs and all other data collected by storm chasers have helped scientists understand hurricanes and tornadoes better.**

**Q** What is a waterspout?

**A** Tornadoes usually travel across land. However, occasionally, tornadoes pass over water. In these cases, the high-speed winds suck in water, creating tall columns of spinning water called waterspouts. These waterspouts are weaker than land tornadoes and occur in warm tropical oceans. However, they are still strong enough to cause huge damage to any boat or ship caught in them.

**▲ Waterspout**
When tornadoes pass over water, they suck the water up into tall spinning columns called waterspouts.

## Try these too...

Earth's Atmosphere (8–9), Seasons and Climate (10–11), Oceans (16–17), Americas (24), Asia (29)

# Americas

The Americas lie in the western hemisphere. Together they cover an area of 42,320,000 square kilometers (16,340,000 square miles), which is a little less than 8.5 percent of the Earth. The two continents are connected by a narrow strip of land called the Isthmus of Panama. Most of South America is in the southern hemisphere. To the west of the Americas lies the Pacific Ocean, and to the the east is the Atlantic Ocean.

## Quick Q's:

**1. Where is Niagara Falls?**

Niagara Falls is on the river Niagara, between Canada and the United States. It is really three falls—the American Falls, the Canadian or Horseshoe Falls and the Bridal Veil Falls. In one minute, more than 168,000 cubic meters (6 million cubic feet) of water falls over its crest.

**2. Which is the highest waterfall in South America?**

Angel Falls on Auyan Tepui river in Venezuela falls 979 meters (3,212 feet). It is the highest waterfall in the world. It is named after James Crawford Angel, who first saw it from his aeroplane in 1933. The local name is Churún Merú, which means Devil's Mouth.

**3. Which is the longest mountain range in South America?**

Stretching for 7,000 kilometers (4,400 miles), the Andes is the longest mountain range in the world. It starts near the equator and goes on almost to Antarctica. In some places, it is 500 kilometers (300 miles) wide.

**Q** Which countries make up North America?

**A** North America is made up of three countries. Canada, the largest, is in the north, followed by the United States of America in the middle and Mexico in the south.

**Q** What are the main geographical regions in North America?

**A** There are four principal geographical regions in North America. These include the Appalachian Mountains (eastern USA) and the Great Plains, which stretch from the Gulf of Mexico in the south to the northern parts of Canada. The other regions are the West, where the Rocky Mountains are found, and beyond the Rockies, the low-lying Great Basin.

**Q** What types of climate are found in South America?

**A** The Pacific coasts of Colombia and Ecuador have a tropical climate, with wet summers and dry winters. The northern coasts of Venezuela and Colombia are dry and prone to droughts. The coastal regions in Peru and northern Chile are also very dry. The cold currents off these shores do not carry moisture. In the Andes mountains there is an alpine climate, and the areas around them are cool. South of the tropic of Capricorn, the climate is temperate—summers are cool and winters are cold. Patagonia in southern Argentina has an almost polar climate.

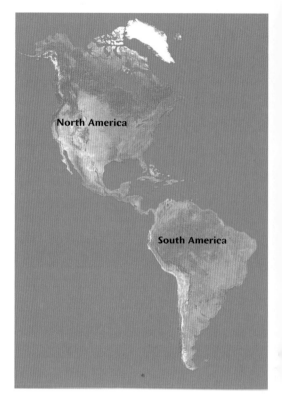

North America

South America

▲ **North and South America**
The third largest continent after Asia and Africa, North America had a population of 514.6 million in 2006. South America is the fourth largest continent. It is about two and a half times the size of Australia.

▼ **Rocky road**
The Rocky Mountains run from north to south through much of the North American continent.

# Australia and Oceania

Oceania is a group of about 10,000 islands that lie in the Pacific Ocean between Asia and America. It includes the continent of Australia. Unlike the other continents, Oceania is a region linked by water rather than land. It was given its name in 1831 by French explorer Dumont d'Urville.

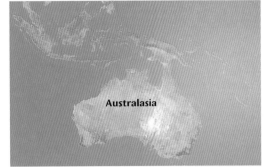

**Australasia**

**Q** Other than Australia, what are the islands included in Oceania?

**A** Oceania has four regions: Micronesia, Melanesia, Polynesia and Australasia. These regions are divided into thousands of islands. Fiji, Indonesia and Papua New Guinea are in Melanesia. Micronesia is a chain of tiny islands that forms the Federated States of Micronesia. The Cook Islands, Samoa and Tonga are in Polynesia. Australia, New Zealand and Christmas Island are part of Australasia. Hawaii, in the middle of the Pacific Ocean, is also part of Oceania.

▲ **An unknown continent**
The early inhabitants of Australia are believed to have come from Southeast Asia about 48,000 years ago.

**Try these too...**

Earth's Atmosphere (8–9), Seasons and Climate (10–11), Mountains, Valleys and Caves (12–13)

**Q** What is the Australian climate like?

**A** Australia is the driest and flattest continent inhabited by people. Most of it is desert, arid land or hummock grasslands. The north of the continent has a warm, tropical climate with rainforests, mangrove swamps and grasslands. The southeast and southwest have a cool and temperate climate. Australia is an island with an area of 7,686,850 square kilometers (2,967,909 square miles). It is surrounded by the Indian and Pacific Oceans. It has a coastline of 25,760 kilometers (16,007 miles) where nearly 90 percent of its population lives.

**Q** Why is Christmas Island so-called?

**A** Christmas Island was given its name by the British captain William Mynors of the ship the *Royal Mary*, because he arrived there on Christmas Day in 1643. This small island in the Indian Ocean is so far from any other landmass that its plants and animals are quite unique. People did not live there earlier, so there has been no human interference. As a result, it is of immense interest to scientists.

## That's some barrier

**The Great Barrier Reef, the longest coral reef in the world, stretches for over 2,000 kilometers (1,250 miles) in the Coral Sea off northeastern Australia. It is made up of 3,000 reefs and 900 islands. The Great Barrier Reef is a precious environmental site because it is home to many thousands of species of fish and marine animals. In 1981, it was made a World Heritage Site. However, life on the reef is still under threat from over-fishing and pollution.**

◀ **Natural beauty**
New Zealand is known for the beauty of its lakes and mountains. The country consists of two large islands, North Island and South Island, and numerous smaller islands.

# Europe

Europe is the sixth of the seven continents in terms of size. It covers 10,390,000 square kilometers (4,010,000 square miles), which is 2 percent of the surface of the Earth. To the north of Europe lies the Arctic Ocean, and to the west, the Atlantic Ocean. To the south, Europe is separated from Africa by the Mediterranean Sea. To the east, the boundary with Asia is not clear, but it is around the Ural Mountains and the Caspian Sea.

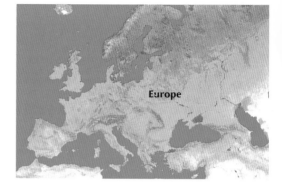

**▲ British Isles**
The United Kingdom is made up of four countries: England, Scotland, Wales and Northern Ireland.

## Quick Q's:

**1. Is the Vatican City a country?**

Vatican City, which is an enclave in Rome, is the world's smallest independent country. It is the seat of the Roman Catholic Church. It is ruled by the pope.

**2. Why is Norway called the land of the midnight Sun?**

One-third of Norway lies north of the Arctic Circle. From May to the end of July, this region has continuous daylight.

**3. Where is Istanbul?**

Istanbul is in northwest Turkey. It is the only city in the world to be in two continents—Europe and Asia. It is divided into two by the Bosporus Strait.

**Q** What is the landscape of Europe like?

**A** Europe is more mountainous toward the south, which also has some of the best beaches, on the Mediterranean coast. The Alps cover parts of Austria, Slovenia, Italy, Switzerland, Liechtenstein, France and Germany. Although the Alps have high peaks like Mont Blanc and Piz Bernina, the highest peak in Europe is Mount Elbrus in Russia, 5,642 meters (18,510 feet), in the Caucasus range. Moving beyond the Alps, the Pyrenees and the Carpathians, the land rolls into the Great European Plain. The British Isles are separated from the rest of the continent by the English Channel and the North Sea.

**▲ Temperate land**
The Gulf Stream that flows in from the Atlantic Ocean keeps northwestern Europe warmer than other places at the same latitude.

**Q** Does Europe have forests?

**A** Centuries ago, about 90 percent of Europe was covered in forest. Now, more than half of this has been felled. However, in countries like Finland, 72 percent of the land is still covered by forests. Evergreen and deciduous forests cover most ground. Conifer forests are found in Scandinavia and parts of Russia and Ukraine. Further north is the taiga region with forests of spruce, birch and pine. The Mediterranean region has cork oak forests, cypress trees and olives.

**◄ Flamenco dancer**
The flamenco of Spain is one of the many traditional dance forms popular in Europe.

**▼ City of canals**
Venice, a city off the coast of northeastern Italy, has canals instead of roads.

# Africa

Africa is the second largest continent in the world. The Romans named it "Africa terra," which means land of the Afri, after a tribe who lived in North Africa. Africa has around 840,000,000 people. It covers about 30,300,000 square kilometers (11,700,000 square miles) including the islands. This is roughly 6 percent of the total surface of the Earth.

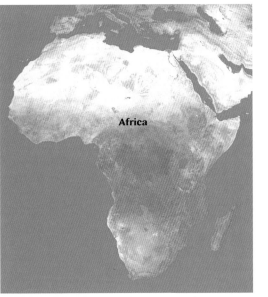

**Africa**

## Q Where can I find Africa on the globe?

A Africa is the only continent straddling the tropic of Cancer, the equator and the tropic of Capricorn. It lies to the south of Europe and the Mediterranean Sea and to the west of Asia, beyond the Red Sea. To its west is the Atlantic Ocean and to its east is the Indian Ocean. It is a long continent, stretching 8,000 kilometers (5,000 miles) from the tip of Tunisia in the north to its most southern point in South Africa, the Cape of Good Hope. It is widest at the center, with 7,400 kilometers (4,600 miles) between its most eastern point in Somalia and its western coast. Africa's coastline is 26,000 kilometers (16,100 miles) long.

## Q What are the major lakes, rivers and mountains of Africa?

A Lakes Victoria, Tanganyika, Albert, Edward and Kivu are the Great Lakes of Africa, in the Great Rift Valley. Lake Victoria covers 69,500 square kilometers (26,836 square miles) and is the world's second largest freshwater lake. The Nile River, at 6,825 kilometers (4,241 miles) long, is the longest river in the world. Other rivers in Africa include the Congo, the Zambezi and the Niger. The highest mountain in Africa is Mount Kilimanjaro in northeastern Tanzania. Kibo is Kilimanjaro's highest peak. It is 5,895 meters (19,341 feet) tall. Although close to the equator, the peak is so high it is covered with snow.

◀ **Many climates**
Africa has several different climate zones. The Sahara keeps the north hot and dry. The center has the rainforests, the southeast has the savannah.

### Try these too...

Earth's Atmosphere (8–9), Seasons and Climate (10–11), Mountains, Valleys and Caves (12–13), Other Landforms (14–15), Oceans (16–17), Volcanoes (18–19)

## What-a-fall!

Victoria Falls, locally called Mosi-oa-Tunya (meaning "smoke that thunders"), is on the Zambezi River between Zambia and Zimbabwe. The falls are about 1.7 kilometers (1 mile) wide and 128 meters (420 feet) high—the largest single sheet of water in the world. In 1855, David Livingstone named the falls after Queen Victoria. They are a World Heritage Site.

▼ **Haven for animals**
The African savannah—now a series of national parks—is home to a huge variety of wild animals.

# The Poles—The Arctic and Antarctica

The North and South Poles are at the two ends of the Earth's axis. The North Pole is the northernmost part of the Earth, and the most southern tip of the Earth is the South Pole, in Antarctica. The Arctic and the Antarctic are the most arid (dry) places on Earth.

## Quick Q's:

**1. Why is 21 June an important day around the Arctic Circle?**

On 21 June or the summer solstice, the Sun does not set north of the Arctic Circle. That is why this area is called the land of the midnight sun. For the local residents, this is a time to celebrate. On the other hand, on 21 December—the winter solstice—the Sun does not rise at all.

**2. What lies below the ice and snow?**

Many minerals have been found in the Arctic, although mining is difficult. Russia and the US have found deposits of coal, copper, nickel, gold, uranium, tungsten, diamonds, natural gas and oil. Antarctica may also be rich in minerals.

**3. Do people live in the Arctic?**

Hunters from Siberia were the first people to live in the Arctic, arriving about 5,000 years ago. The Inuit of North America, the Greenlanders, the Lapps of western Europe, and some groups of people in Russia and Siberia live in the Arctic. They hunt, fish and keep herds of reindeer.

**Q** What is the Arctic?

**A** From the air, the Arctic would look like a blob of ice surrounded by ocean and rock, with a scattering of islands. The Arctic Circle is an imaginary line around the Earth which represents the southern limit of the Arctic region. The average summer temperature north of the Arctic Circle does not rise above 10 °C (50 °F).

**Q** Which countries are in the Arctic?

**A** Parts of Canada, Alaska (the largest state in the USA), Russia, Norway, Sweden, Finland, Iceland and Greenland lie within the Arctic circle. The Arctic landmass is made up of mountains, plateaus and tundra plains. The tundra is flat and marshy and covered by permafrost (permanent ground frost). The sea in the Arctic, known as the Arctic Ocean, is frozen over for much of the year.

▲ **Discovering the south pole**
For centuries, people kept searching for the "Southern Continent." Antarctica was finally discovered in 1819.

**Q** Does it rain in the Arctic?

**A** The climate in the Arctic is polar. It has a short, cool summer and long, freezing winter. In the outer edges of the Arctic—the tundra—the average summer temperature is between 0 and 10 °C (32–50 °F). Among the ice caps, it is below 0 °C (32 °F) throughout the year, and there is a permanent cover of snow. Most of the precipitation (rainfall) is frozen and falls as snow, but it does occasionally rain.

▼ **Continent of ice**
Huge cliffs of ice are found at the edge of the Antarctic continent.

# Asia

Asia is the largest continent in the world. It spreads over an area of 44,390,000 square kilometers (17,139,000 square miles). This is 8.7 percent of the total area on Earth, or 29.8 percent of the total landmass. Over 3.5 billion—six out of every ten—people live in Asia. Except for a few of its islands, Asia is in the northern hemisphere—north of the equator.

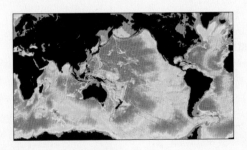

**▶ Large and populous**
The continent of Asia accommodates about 60 percent of the world's total population.

**Q** Who are Asia's neighbors?

**A** To its west, Asia borders Europe. If you drew an imaginary line along the Ural mountains to the Caspian Sea, the Black Sea and the Aegean Sea, it would be the western border of Asia. Asia has the Arctic Ocean in the north, the Indian Ocean in the south, and the Pacific Ocean in the east.

**Q** What is the landscape of Asia like?

**A** Asia is home to Mount Everest, the highest point on Earth and to the Dead Sea, the lowest surface on Earth. Along the coast and in river valleys are fertile plains. They include the valleys of the Yangtze and Hwang Ho rivers in China; the Ganges, Brahmaputra and the Indus rivers in south Asia; and the Tigris and Euphrates rivers in west Asia. The Yangtze is the longest river in Asia, covering 6,380 kilometers (3,964 miles). The highest mountain ranges in the world are in Asia— the Himalayas, Hindu Kush, Kunlun and Tien Shan mountains.

## Sitting on a seabed

During the Paleozoic and Mesozoic eras, 570 million to 65 million years ago, the Tethys Sea covered most of what is Asia and parts of Europe. The Indian subcontinent broke off from Africa and drifted toward the northeast. As the land pushed north, it crumpled and folded to form the Himalaya mountains. Gradually, the islands of eastern Asia, such as Japan and Taiwan, began to grow. The plates that make up Asia are still moving and settling, which makes this region prone to volcanic activity, earthquakes and natural disasters such as the 2004 tsunami that devastated many countries around the Indian Ocean.

**▾ Modern cities**
Many Asian cities such as Dubai (seen here), are full of high rise buildings.

**◀ International tastes**
The cuisines of China, India and Japan are famous all over the world.

## Try these too...

Earth's Atmosphere (8–9), Seasons and Climate (10–11), Mountains, Valleys and Caves (12–13), Other Landforms (14–15)

# Index